BOOK TWO

by Ann Bryant

GW00645311

For Jayne Aspinall
Great musician, great friend

Illustrations by
Paul Selvey, John Good Holbrook Ltd.

Design and Typesetting by
John Good Holbrook Ltd.

Music Setting by
Barnes Music Engraving Ltd.

Published 1998

© **International Music Publications Limited**
Southend Road, Woodford Green,
Essex IG8 8HN, England

EXCLUSIVE DISTRIBUTORS
International Music Publications Limited
Southend Road, Woodford Green,
Essex IG8 8HN, England

International Music Publications Limited
25 rue d'Hauteville, 75010 Paris, France

International Music Publications GmbH, Germany
Marstallstraße 8, D-80539 München, Germany

Nuova Carisch S.p.A.
Via Campania, 12
20098 San Giuliano Milanese - Milano, Italy

Danmusik
Vognmagergade 7, DK-1120 Copenhagen K,
Denmark

Warner/Chappell Music Australia Pty Ltd.
3 Talavera Road, North Ryde,
New South Wales 2113, Australia

Warner Bros. Publications
16800 NW 48th Avenue, Miami Fl 33014, USA

Caring for the Environment
This book has been produced with special regard to the environment. We have insisted on the use of acid-free, neutral-sized paper made from
pulps which have not been elemental bleached and have sought assurance that the pulp is farmed from sustainable forests.

More fun learning the piano...

Hi Keyclub kids, and welcome to Keyclub Book Two.
Just as promised, you're going to find this book packed with exciting things to do and play. Look out for a whole new bunch of great characters and places as you travel through Keyland and have more fun learning the piano.

Where to find what ...

KEYCLUB Kids

At a moderate speed

mf Key - club Kids can en - ter Key - club a - ny time, night or day.

Up!

Keys can o - pen doors to pla - ces, and to pie - ces you can play.

3

Flea jump up

A new note for R.H.
High C

high Cs

What's on the Menu?

Quite slowly

mf Ham   and   eggs   and   sau - sage and   chips.   Jack - et   spuds   and   bis - cuits and   dips.

Up!

Fine

Ham-bur-gers,   beef bur-gers,   hot dish-es,   cold dish-es,   cheese bur-gers,   choice bur-gers,   fried fish and   chips.

Down!

Up!

D.C. al Fine

④

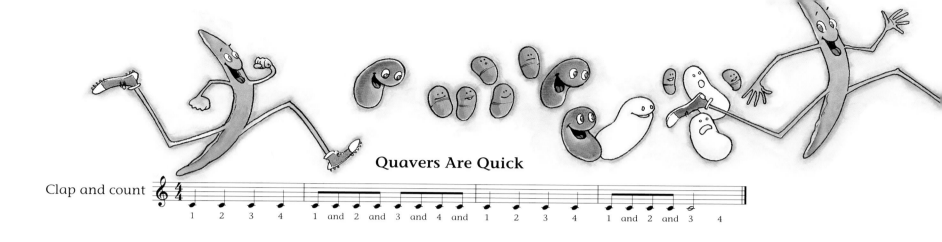

Quavers Are Quick

Clap and count

1 2 3 4 1 and 2 and 3 and 4 and 1 2 3 4 1 and 2 and 3 4

Beans Are In!

At a moderate speed

mf

Beans are in! Beans are in! Kid-ney, run-ner, broad and but-ter, beans are in!

Whe-ther they are round or long and string-y thin, kid-ney, run-ner, broad and but-ter, beans are in!

Up!

Quavers come in pairs

Clap and count

1 and 2 and 3 and 4 and 1 2 3 4 1 and 2 and 3 and 4 and 1 2 3 4

Clap and count

1 2 1 2 1 and 2 and 1 2 1 2 1 and 2 1 2 and 1 2

Marching Muffin Men

Quite fast

mf

Jaunt - ing | gin - ger breads | jive on the | jam - jars. | Twirl - ing | tof - fee mall-ows | twist and | tap.

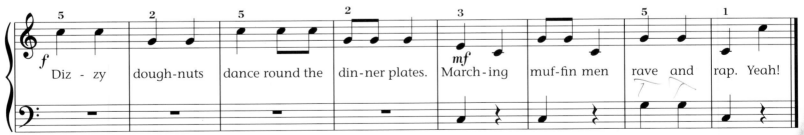

f

Diz - zy | dough-nuts | dance round the | din-ner plates. | *mf* March - ing | muf-fin men | rave and | rap. Yeah!

Beetles' Barlines
Put the barlines in the right place.

Tell your teacher the letter names of the notes in exercise three.

Frank The Frog

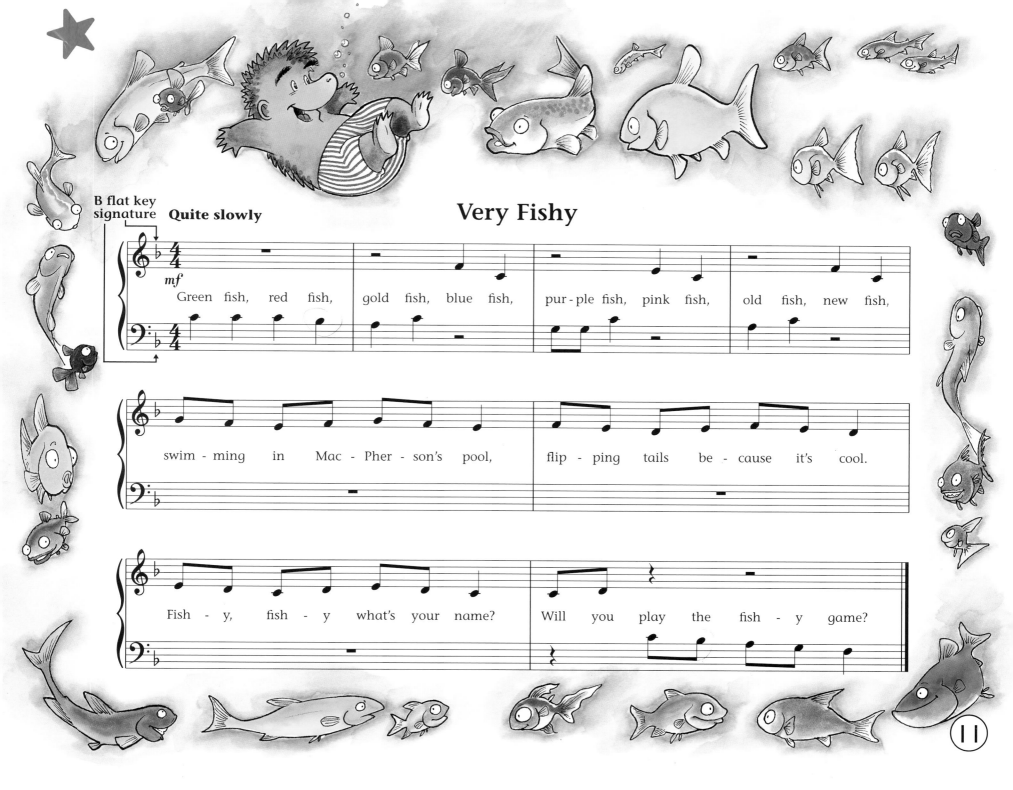

Very Fishy

Water Sports

Slowly

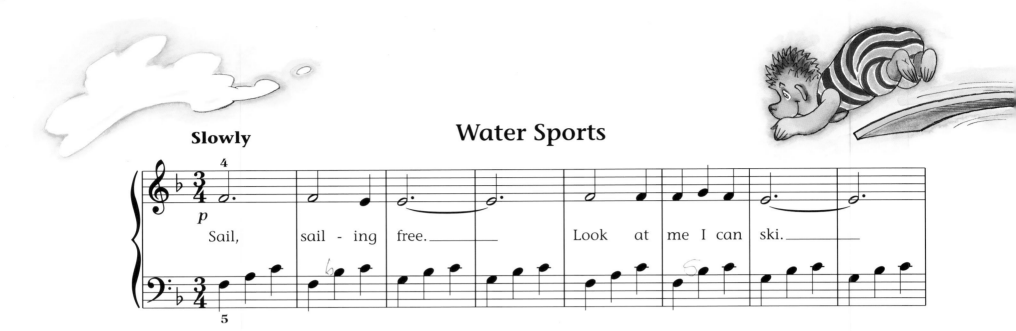

Sail, sail - ing free._____ Look at me I can ski._____

Surf, surf - ing, surf - ing free. Swim, swim in the sea._____

mf

rit. dim.

Quick over!

STICKER HERE

12

King of the Wolves

Quite slowly

_mf_

Wil - bur wolf is the king of the woods. He lives a - lone in his lair. If he

hears a sound when he's prowl-ing a - round, his growl sounds _rit._ just like 'Who's there?!'

13

Wilbur in Disguise

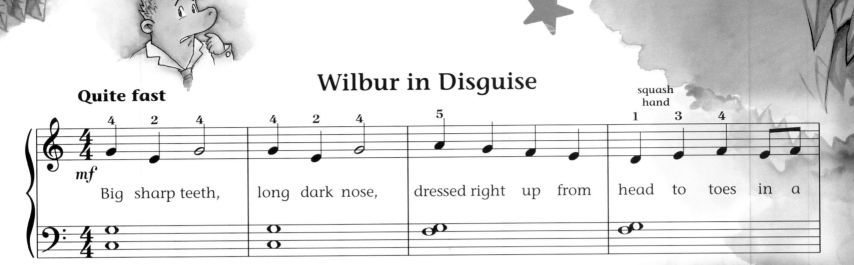

Quite fast

mf

Big sharp teeth, long dark nose, dressed right up from head to toes in a

night shirt, Gran-ny's shirt, nast-y gleam-ing eyes.

Is it Wil-bur in dis-guise?

Woodlouse's "What?" Page

What are these? _____

What is this? > _____

What is this interval? _____

What note is this? _____

What note is this? _____

What does this mean? *dim.* _____

What is this? _____

What is this sign at the start of a piece? _____

What are two notes played together like this called? _____

What does this mean? **D.C. al Fine** _____

What does this mean? _____

What does this mean? *rit.* _____

The Three Bears' House

1st time: **Slow** 2nd time: **Medium** 3rd time: **Fast**

1. In the mid-dle of the woods, there's a fun-ny lit - tle place. In the

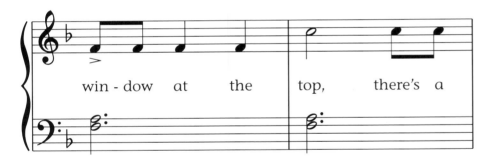

win - dow at the top, there's a

grow - ly dad - dy bear's face.

Verse 2.
In the middle of the woods,
There's a funny little place.
In the window underneath,
There's a smiley mummy bear's face.

Verse 3.
In the middle of the woods,
There's a funny little place.
In the window at the side,
There's a cheeky baby bear's face.

Roly Poly Rabbit

Quite slowly

mf

With a | swish, swish, swish and a | swirl, swirl, swirl, the | leaves all rus-tle when a | vole takes a stroll, and the

tree tops sway as the | birds all play, and the

dim.

ro - ly po - ly rab-bit tries to | hide in a hole.

A new note for L.H.

Digging and Tunnelling

At a moderate speed

p

Down un-der ground there is | dark-ness all | round, and the | moles | live | there | yeah!

Dig-ging and | tun-nel-ling, | dig-ging and | tun-nel-ling, | *crescendo* tak-ing their | turn to keep | watch ev-'ry | where.

Mole Patrol

Like a march

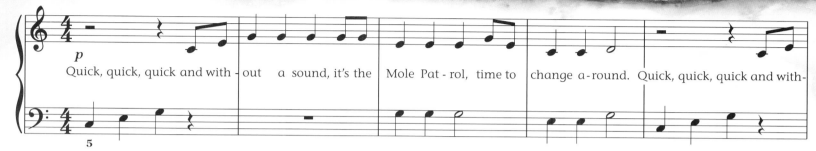

Quick, quick, quick and with-out a sound, it's the Mole Pat-rol, time to change a-round. Quick, quick, quick and with-

-out a sound, there's a new guard un-der-ground. Up a-bove there are an-gry sighs, as the

Fine

rich black soil spoils the gar-den green. 'One more mole hill and I'll go mad! Such a mess, I've ne-ver seen!'

crescendo

D.C. al Fine

19

Wayne The Worm

Moles Are Pests!

Briskly

Dig, dig, dig, heave, heave, heave, what a love-ly ear-thy mound. Dig, dig, dig,

heave, heave, heave, oh, what fun liv-ing un-der-ground. Stomp, stomp, stomp, poke, poke, poke,

Fine

moles are pests go-ing to and fro. Stomp, stomp, stomp, poke, poke, poke, moles are pests liv-ing down be-low.

D.C. al Fine

21

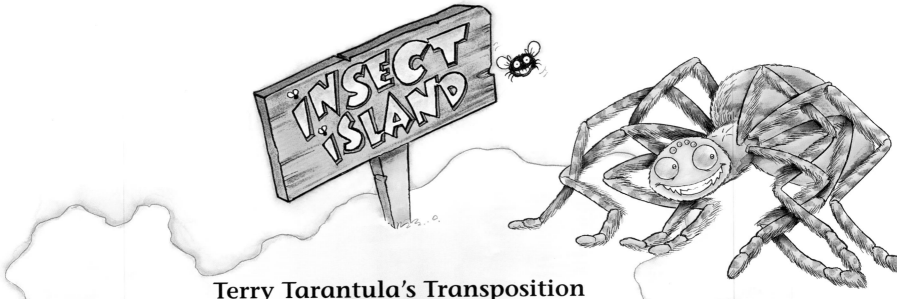

Terry Tarantula's Transposition

Fill in the missing notes of the piece below so it has exactly the same tune as the piece above, only starting on F instead of C. Look at the steps, skips and frog jump above, and make each interval the same below.

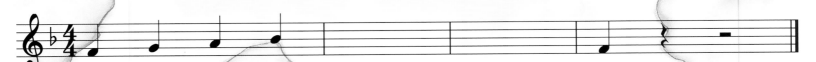

Put a ring around any note you have never come across before.
There should be two (both the same). What letter name do you think they have?
Turn over to see if you are right.

TWINS' TOWN

A new note for L.H. and R.H.
D and B

Olympic jump

Roll Up! Roll Up!

Quite fast

mf
Roll up, roll up,   roll up, roll up!   *crescendo* This is where the   fun be - gins.

f
See - ing dou - ble,   see - ing dou - ble,   *dim.* see - ing twins and   twins and twins!

Dipperty and Dopperty

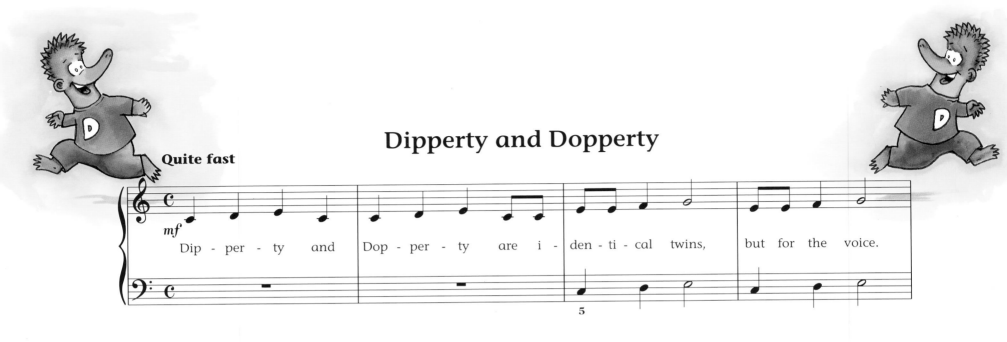

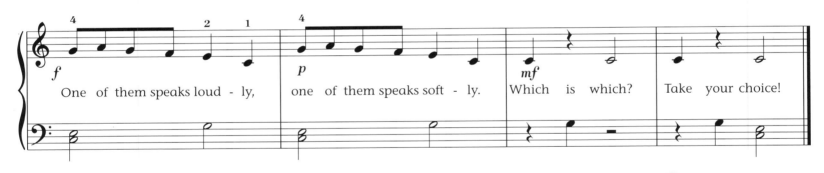

Carie and Mary Quite Contrary

At a moderate speed

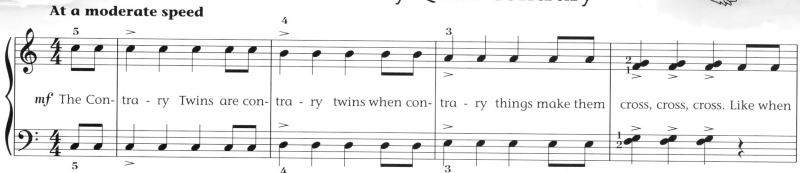

mf The Con- tra - ry Twins are con- tra - ry twins when con- tra - ry things make them cross, cross, cross. Like when

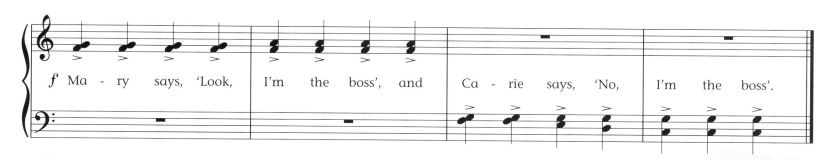

f Ma - ry says, 'Look, I'm the boss', and Ca - rie says, 'No, I'm the boss'.

What's the Difference?

A new note for R.H.

B flat

B flat   B flat   B flat

At a moderate speed

f   Is it Kel-ly Ann?   Is it Em-ma Jane?   *mf* I can't tell the differ-ence, can you tell the differ-ence?

Kel — ly?   Em — ma?   *rit.* *dim.* What is your name?

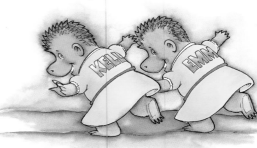

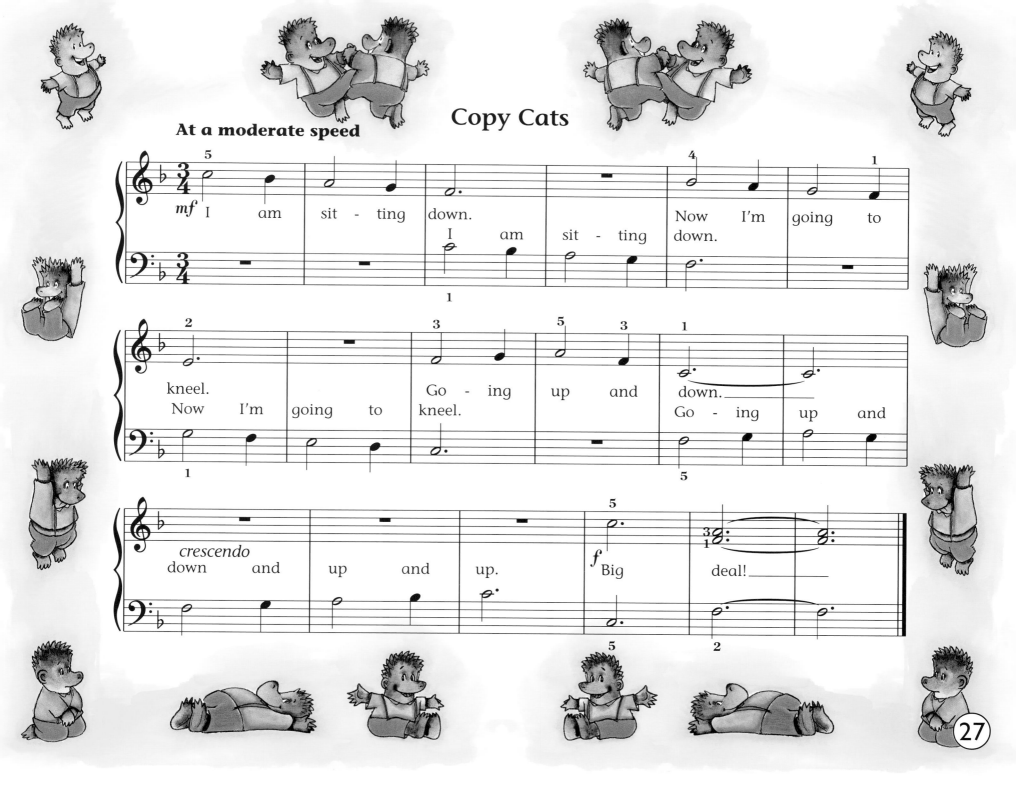

Copy Cats

At a moderate speed

INFO-CHECK!

Notes you know

Intervals you know

Step up Skip down Flea jump up Frog jump up Kangaroo jump down Olympic jump up Rocket Sky dive

You also know...

dim. or diminuendo - get gradually quieter

cresc. or crescendo - get gradually louder

3 note chord

anacrusis or upbeat

quavers

accent

B flat key signature

28

A new note for L.H.

F sharp

Grovelly and Gravelly

At a moderate speed

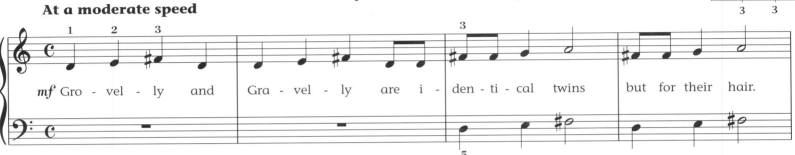

mf Gro - vel - ly and Gra - vel - ly are i - den - ti - cal twins but for their hair.

One of them has blonde hair, one of them has black hair. Real - ly weird! What a pair!

STICKER HERE

30

Incy Wincy's Intervals!

Can you write in the correct note to make the interval it says?

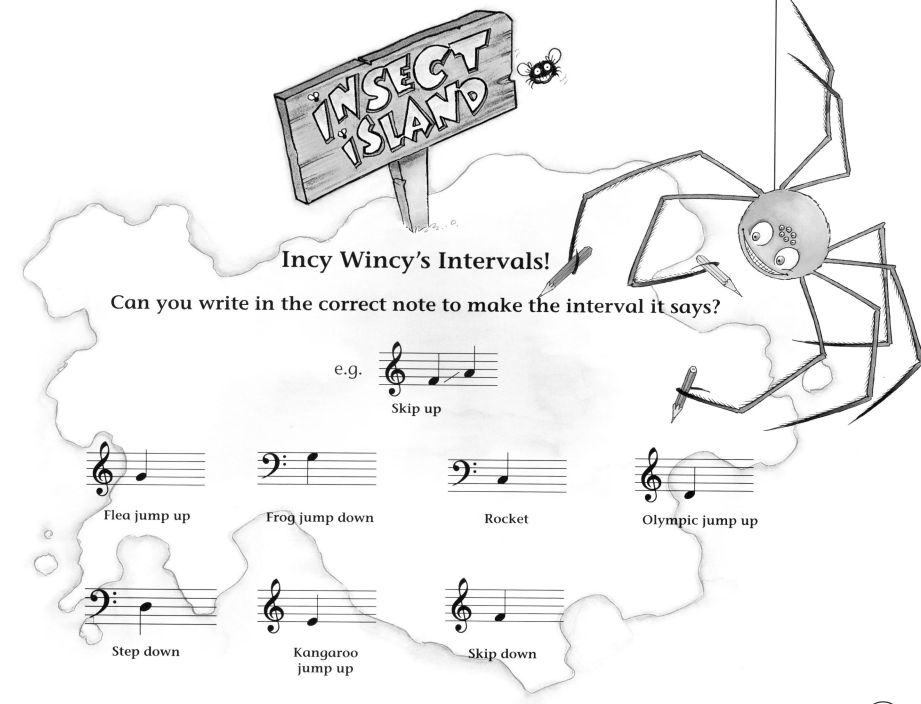

e.g.

Skip up

Flea jump up

Frog jump down

Rocket

Olympic jump up

Step down

Kangaroo
jump up

Skip down

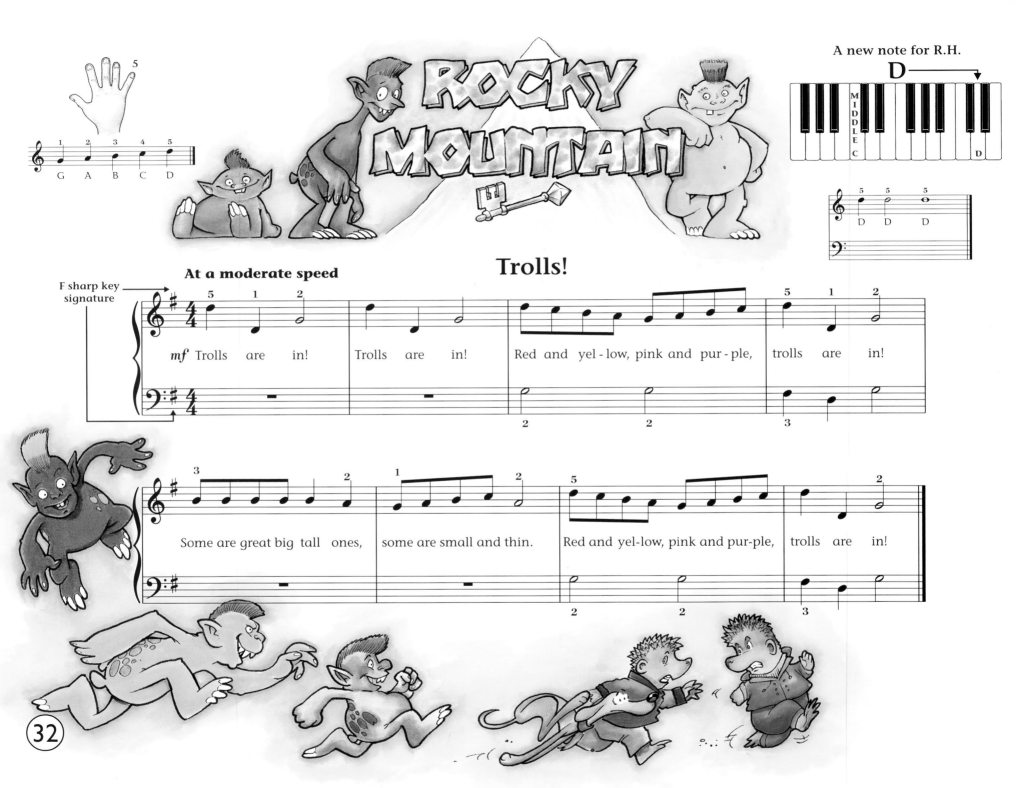

Up and Down the Mountainside

Racing Round the Mountain

At a moderate speed

They'll be ra - cing round the moun - tain just you wait. They'll be

ra - cing round the moun-tain just you wait. They'll be ra - cing round the moun-tain,

ra - cing round the moun-tain, ra - cing round the moun-tain just you wait.

The Grogs' Grunge Dance

Two More Transpositions from Terry T.

An octave means eight notes apart (like a skydive or rocket).
Fill in the missing notes of piece 2 so that it is all an octave lower than piece 1. We have started you off.

1.

2.

Fill in the missing notes of piece 4 so that it is all an octave higher than piece 3.
We have started you off.

3.

4.

Mountain Fireworks

Marvin the Mountain Guide

At a moderate speed

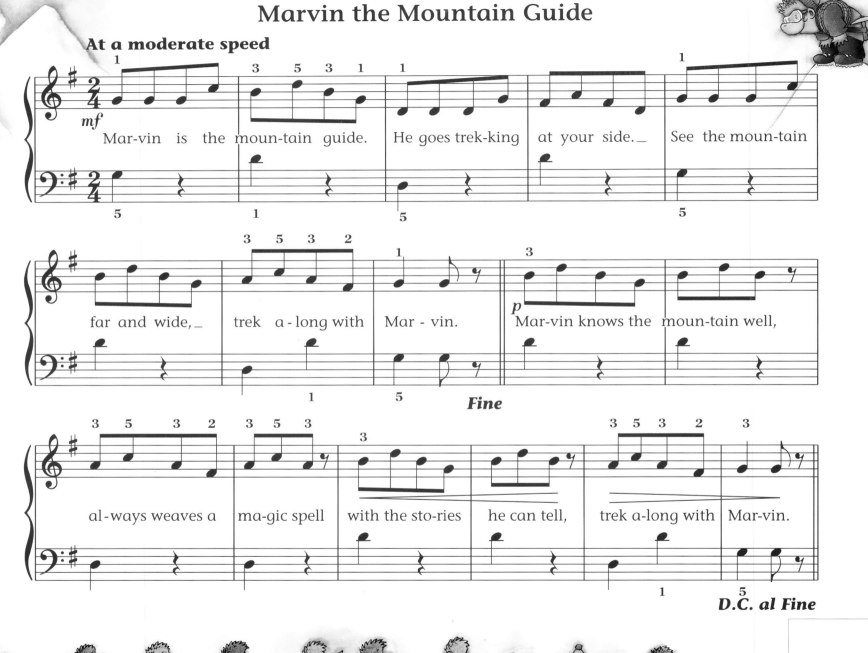

A new note for L.H.

B

A Tale to be Told

Slowly and gently

What A Cheat!

Fairly fast

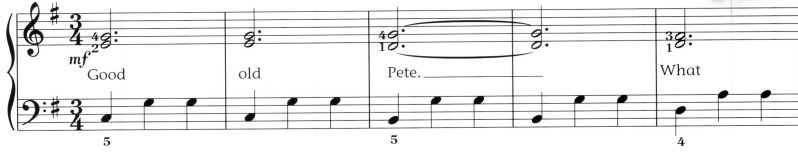

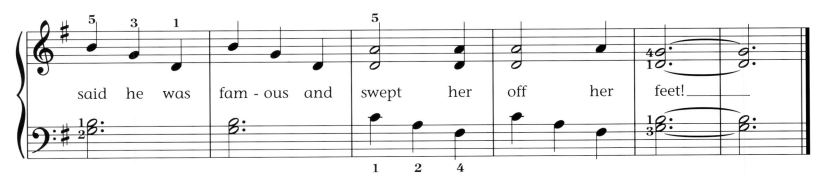

40

Wasp's Words

Make words by writing in the letter names of the notes

Pete - The Roller Blading King

At a moderate speed

Slide, slide, roll-er blad-ing king. Slide, slide,

roll - er blad-ing king. No - bo - dy can beat him roll - er blad-ing

Fine

Pete. No - bo - dy can bring him to de - feat.

D.C. al Fine

Pete - Roller Blading Even Faster!

At a moderate speed

Working Hard at the Palace
(Teacher's Part)

Working Hard at the Palace
(Pupil's Part)

At a moderate speed

Dust-ing, dust-ing high and low and sweep-ing, sweep-ing to and fro and rush-ing, rush-ing

on the go, we're work-ing at the pal-ace. All day long, we ne-ver stop,

till we're feel-ing fit to drop, Mis-ter, Miss and Mas-ter Mop, work-ing at the pal-ace.

Notes you now know

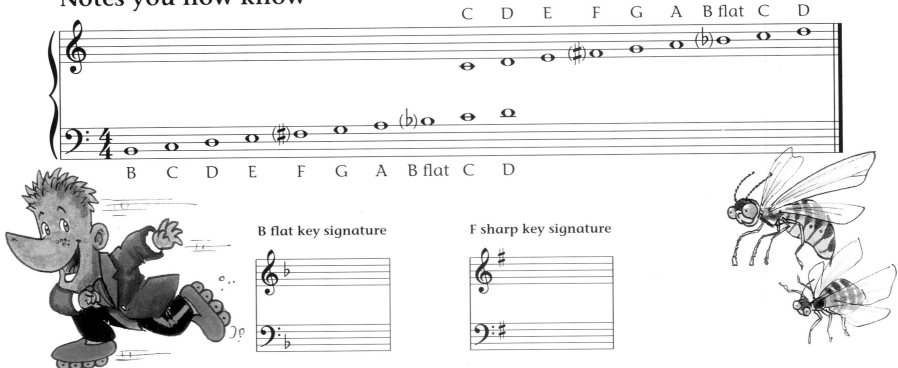

C   D   E   F   G   A   B flat   C   D

B   C   D   E   F   G   A   B flat   C   D

B flat key signature

F sharp key signature

Intervals

Step up   Skip down   Flea jump up   Frog jump down   Kangaroo jump up   Olympic jump up   Rocket   Skydive

Time Values

 = quavers

Two together make
one crotchet count

♪ = quaver

Half a crotchet
count

𝄾 = quaver rest

Dynamics or changes in volume

crescendo or ———————— = get gradually louder

diminuendo or ———————— = get gradually softer

8va = play an octave higher

> = accent

anacrusis

Well Done!

This certifies that

_____

has successfully completed Book Two
of the KEYCLUB piano course

_____ Teacher

_____ Date